THE MUD ROOM

Joanna Solfrian

MadHat Press
Cheshire, Massachusetts

MadHat Press
PO Box 422, Cheshire MA 01225

The Library of Congress has assigned
this edition a Control Number of
2020933967

ISBN 978-1-941196-99-1 (paperback)

Cover design by Marc Vincenz
Cover image by Dylan Haigh
Author photo by David Quinn
Book design by MadHat Press

www.MadHat-Press.com

for Olive and Willa

and for Scott and our four who've flown

Table of Contents

1.

2.

3.

1.

The Moon Has Come to My Window, So I Practice Gratitude

I am grateful for the small
children, their clamor as they run down the dirt road,
the penumbras around them,

their bright braids and weeping knees.

Invisible inside them
is a mirror for angels, so that the temporarily holy
can recognize themselves.

Their brows are a grave where ideas rest.
The mothers kiss them there,
as I just did, bedside,
and the ideas move.

In this way, we are all free.

Joanna Solfrian

Desire

When every cup is filled with wine,
we lose the capacity for desire.

The first gasp after the womb:
the mouth-to-mouth of God's desire?

Defenestrate the cups! Come to the garden at night.
Don't be demure, the grass is already naked. Desire:

notes float from the guitar to the infant's throat.
She wails them back, black with desire.

Forget the dog, the groceries. He can defecate
in the yard; you can subsist on desire.

Ode to the Subway

Your glass eyes are a thought
through which
your conductor watches,
uncrimping his tin horn
behind him.

Your wheezing and
knocking and clattering are
an old man
throwing his cane
down a flight of stairs.

Rest for a minute,
muzzled soldier!

Your perfect-third bell—
bing bong—
and your warm innards
are a relief

the way tragedy
is a relief
after too much longing.

We are a party
of uninvited guests.
O woman, stop injecting
strange liquids

into your lips—
leave the taut shine
to the September tomato.
Sir, I love your tattoos
and your stout belly
which rubs against
my arm.
Thank you for looking
for my pen cap!

And you, drowsy ungendered
child in goose down,
hatted, scarved, and
mittened,
your mother's bosom
is right there!

Let's sit in our tin suit
with our indented buttons
and make
digestive noises.
Stillness is impossible—
the homeless man
ticks his eyes—
he is hungry
and panicked.

O caterpillar,
where is thy leaf?

The laborer gifted
his lungs,
his mother-grown
palms
and blew
your veins out
with dynamite
so you could
hurtle us
to school
to work
to love
with a galvanic
knowledge
of the underworld.

You are a stranger
to vertical ascent
unlike the rest of us
who keep looking
up as if
the departed's
dangling feet
are within reach.

Your orphan lurchings
don't need liftoff—
in fact, you will
exhale me
like an
Aristotelian particle—
and if these pages
drifted onto
your tracks
you would
blacken them
with your evacuative
circumference,
spit them to the gods,
on your way
someplace
other,
someplace better
than the vatic
potentialities
of ink.

In Our Time Together

In our time together
a wide road was cleared
and trees cut down
to make room for new houses.

You can see into them now,
their people, their movements
and modest chandeliers ...
you can see into them
the way you cannot see
God or his washing of hands.

Even though we walked that road
for meditation,
lungs,
cells,
our feet didn't make much difference,

and you left.
Now it's all over.
We're all gone but two,
and when the two write
the ink rearranges and somehow
our pleas come out as

how are the children
and *not much here.*

You Have Been Gone So Long

You have been gone so long your form has stopped
clicking across cobblestones in some alien, conjured land.
I do not see the hem of your gray skirt eddying
around a corner. No matter how I tenderly I ask,
the pond does not retain your reflection and offers
only the dull vowels of clouds. Your means of sight,
if you have any, does not absorb the cities I have lived in—
their skyscrapers and cranes, their human lift—
nor my synapses, which fire every thought upwards,
as if you were sleeping in the trees. The garden compels
me to rip weeds, to seek your fingernail, a sickle
upon which to sacrifice a soul, though there is
no fingernail, there is no soul.

You have been gone so long you do not know
that from my deep core I have ignited
life five times, made it whole and beating twice.
Your being is infinitely zero. The vegetables
on the counter know only me as their executioner.
You do not know my children, who climb
onto my lap and squeeze my breasts
into a shape only they recognize. Even the gray sky
belongs to the ocean, which waves, folds, and continually
feeds on itself. You have been gone so long
I have stopped remembering you.
It is such work to hear your laugh full of bells.

In church I am told you are with me.
I sit here now in the sun and dust and I open,
dumbly, like a hymnal. What is there to praise?
Your prodigal absence, the earthen form
it takes, which is akin not only to roots
but to the hollows the roots make
after they've grown away.

Joanna Solfrian

Grape

Inanimate objects, we are told, move. Their electrons orbit a nucleus the size of a discarded thought. I stare at the table, and its legs don't bend down to pick up the grape that has just rolled off it. The *grape* moved. To my eye, it's now still. It too has moving parts, the way gray toenails and grayer lips have moving parts. The mind is an eye with legs. The neighbors haven't moved in yet. The wars have been over for years but of course still move, especially through the mother-husks. The wind shows us its clear waist when it turns sideways to squeeze by. The mother rims her eyes with black pencil so no evil moves in. The mind moves from idea to pen. The pen moves, sometimes. The heart, always, until no, and then, submittingly, yes, when fire says so. Fire says so when it ignites. Fire is neither animate nor inanimate: it's all forgiveness and tongue—but that grape. It's still sitting there.

The Trunk

My old lover mailed a trunk with golden fasteners.
Inside was a scarlet gown with a black velvet sash.
I slipped into it, and the sash morphed into a pair of snakes,
which wound around my neck and knotted.
The mirror reflected their bright fangs
and four drops of venom, warm on my collarbone.
I charmed the snakes into a black-linked chain
and the venom into salt. I strung the salt
on the chain and embedded a fang in each crystal.
The trunk is light when I mail it back, the necklace
hardly a whit. The gown spreads nicely
into a tablecloth, at which my new lover and I sit.

Joanna Solfrian

1990, For Richard

One Sunday, after church:
no one home but him.
We talked books, words,
his father, who had left.

We climbed out his bedroom
window onto the porch
roof. To have something
to tend, he smoked.

I know I must take care
to remember this. The silence,
the shingles' small stones,
the blue vein in his hand.

Ode to Salt

In you live
prisms, the hidden
spectra of the great
gray Pacific,
infinitesimal
cliffs
that cleave
to the jogger's
breasts.

You are at once
clear
and opaque,
like the heavily
muscled
old boyfriend.

Your jagged kingdoms
on a loaf
of bread
cure the yeast
of its bloated
desire
and facilitate
an earthen
crust
that protests
the knife.

When I slice
your playground,
I sacrifice
my thumb
so that
the tears
of my body
can mate
with the tears
of your tide.
When you scatter,

I wet my
opposable god
and in my mouth
millennia
dissolve.
On my tongue
you howl
for your
evaporated Eden,
your mud-
mother's
fecund warmth—
your sting
is the ocean's
rebuke

for my crawling
out of it.

Indeed,
it is possible
your mute
tectonic
heaves
are wiser than
the ocean's
lusty spindrift,
but I prefer
those cubic
souvenirs from
the grit of
simple
work
on my skin,
so that in
the hotel room
when I arrive,

damp in lycra,
panting,
there is something
of your blessed
infinity
to kiss.

Love Poem

Grateful, I wake to cold sun
and snow on the boughs.
The children are curled
in their beds. You snore
sonorously beside me, warm
on your planet of sleep.
There is no cat. There is no dog.
The fern turns one dead stalk
to the window, like a courtier
who has taken off his hat
and forever bows to a lady.

I place a hand on my belly
and think on its caverns,
on what grows or does not
grow there. I turn to you,
my valentine, who commits
to sleep in a manner I have
no knowledge of, and wrap
my foot around yours,
leaving the rest of you un-
tethered. In case you want
to go far.

The Mud Room

for Beth, in memoriam

When I taste water, I taste the stream it came from
and the loins of the man picnicking next to it.

The self swells over and over. Yesterday, I came from
a preacher and a pianist, tomorrow, the balloon

at the end of a boy's string. The room we come from
is the miracle we seek. All along we've been walking

on top of the earth, but the gods come from
within it. If you know the mud room of the world,

you know the creation space, the half-light, all that came from
a pair of eyes and a sudden yes.

Beware, Jo. The tailor's stitching identities. Where he comes
        from,
anyone's fair game. He threads an eye on each sleeve,

so that when the friend must return to where she came from,
she'll see the road and where it goes.

19

Psalm Ghazal I

Why are You so far from my kneeling thoughts?
For the length of my days, will this be so?

Anger gives iron to the blood. Without it,
we'd have no strength to lift up goodness.

Count the fingers on your right hand.
That many more times than Christ you've tracked 'round the
    sun.

God made the trees and the trees are the wind's harp.
What song will you choose for your heart's dialogue?

When you are buried, love, the dust will sing out;
the flowers will cup no bitterness from your bones.

Visitants

The house lists
drunk on moonlight

I lie awake
too much wine

My heart flashes like scissors
lunatic victor

Three feet into sleep
the spouse, the children

In a far-off country
starving children are translated

as *fluttering sparrows*
I look out the window

The dark oak stands
nest after nest after—

to whose god
were the stars speaking

when they flung
their fractured light?

Breakfast

My children do not want to know their origin.

I protest:—Let me tell you! There's an egg, a very tiny
one, and something called sperm, which is—
*We know, Ma, you told us already. They mix
and a baby starts growing.*—But there's more!
The younger one rolls her eyes. The older slides
her cereal bowl to the other end of the table.

There's clay, and a hand of God.
There are specks of stardust, a flame, and a wheel.
You can't see them but you can feel them in your belly.
There's a scar from your own mother: a tiny circle,
from the tether that held you to her, and it opens.
Do you remember?

They are chomping their Rice Krispies and do not hear.
But when I kiss their heads their skull plates move,
and they look up and press my cheek, damp with tears.

2.

Travel

Elsewhere, the sea is the floor of the sky,
but here, the sea is the roof of the underworld.

Tiger rays ruffle the sand with aconsonant travel
and collect messages from the dead.

When the ray is still, he is deciding
which messages to tell and which to bury.

A girl floats on the surface with one ear
tipped downward—

she can hear who will die next
but hasn't the words to tell you.

Joanna Solfrian

Waiting for the Bus, Columbia Street, Brooklyn, the Day After the Writer Jumped Off the Staten Island Ferry

for Spalding Gray

I've left the dishes submerged in the sink and the feeling is
mutual. All this hovering and bits still cling. A shopkeeper
nods to me in English. The brown glass of the bus stop smushes
the light. Where's the bus—oh, hello, sparrow. Harangue that
rind of bread. Now hop away, little casket of feathers. No bus.
A subterranean rumble wiggles my legs like the fat machine
at that carnival—where *was* that? Boom crane. The container
yards go on Containing Things. Joy. Looking for joy … the sky
is white-cold and unabashedly bright. There's my foot, a cloud
stuck in a puddle. [Sniff.] Decades of milk spills and soot and
then water, there's the water, if you separate the particles you
can smell it. Regular, brackish, salt, it's all ocean eventually.
No bus. The explanation: he's not crying, not drowning. He's
simply letting the salt in his ducts become coextensive with
the salt in the channel—the bus! Ah, aluminum tube! Maybe
eight blocks down, bellowing like a top-heavy Baptist. The
sun bounces off its eyes. Sixish blocks. The shopkeeper hangs
a sign in his window. Cough. Cough. Three blocks. There
was something about a depression with claws. Yes, a car crash
and a dented skull. Two blocks. Where's my MetroCard …
notebook … tissues … one—the door spit-sighs open there it
is, shame—he'd said *thank you for helping with the show come
out with my friends we really owe you a drink* and I begged off

26

... *exams tomorrow.* Truth? I was a lake-eyed co-ed with a dead mom and no I.D. Under the mouth of the sky the sparrow, again with the sparrow. And then boom, in my head: its death. The sparrow's, I mean. Not yours. Its death will be dry, competent, while yours ... we are driving by your water now. It is vast and gray and mute. Someone saw you on the ferry, you know. We are driving by your water. People are looking for you. Someone saw you on the ferry. Your wife was on the radio. We are driving by the water which you are under right now. The rest of us only plunge our—and this is supposed to mean we are saved?

Joanna Solfrian

Call Ownership and the Rats Laugh

The cloud's eye is not yours, nor the ecstasy
of a wing making a ladder of air.

You do not sing of mathematics,
of the pattern of an infinite decimal.

Of the heart you know nothing. Only its chambers,
the bed in each one ... a lover, a father, a mother, empty ...

yours is the earth, the stuff of roots, of grubs
and their subterranean riots, all that gasket-chewing.

Yours are the absurd notions of termites
who build mud-veins on the outside of trunks.

Jo, one day you will laugh at what you tried to hold
in your hand, then someone will open a door.

Ode to a Pigeon

O wingèd proletariat
rap-nodding
greetings,
I mostly
love you.

You've donned
epaulets
of molten steel.
On your coat
ripple the gray
waters
of the Atlantic
at sunrise.
You strut
in an utter
blush.

You were cloud-born
to land.
You are a
magicianless
dove.
No matter,
I will look
for your
magic.

Joanna Solfrian

You find nooks
others pass by.
You attend
to the scooped-out
dreams of
the gargoyle
and to the base
angle of the
isosceles
pediment.

Professor,
we must make
a place
at the table
for honesty.
People can't
stand you.
Your persistence
for the potential
abundance
of crumbs
and your lack
of standards
for pooping—
frankly,
we're jealous.
We insist on

fist-sized flour goods
and porcelain.

I am sorry,
beautiful
commoner,
parson of
daffodils!

Come here
with your
caramel
stutter, you
monocular
Pollock.
Friend,
I have
something
to thank you
for this little
song.

Don't Come to Me With Your Whole Body

Don't come to me with your whole body.
Don't buy acres of arabica bush
and hire laborers to dry its fruit.
Please, if you must kiss me,
don't do it passionately, with your hand
in the vines of my hair.

Give me a single finger
and trace a map on my lips.
Give me a cup of coffee in a white cup.
The way the withered leaves give whispers,
give me your mouth.

Then we can travel anywhere
and make a great big ruckus.

Anniversary

The outcomes of our love lie in their bed,
sleep-tangled and yeast-warm from the guitar.
The stars overwhelm their dome, the mangroves
drip their branches down into roots and thus

over years walk the earth. You & I have walked as well,
more quickly—there is bread to buy, and rent.
Our hearts have few bruises but they are
deeply blue. Who knows the occasion for upending

the silence, for saying yes to all—yes
to the dried-up dreams in the bedroom corner,
the unborn dreams in the wood-thrush wing,
the sacred dreams of our love, whom God twice-

molded around bones in the manner of rivers?
Whatever the occasion, there was one,
and I, the lunatic, press it now, and again,
to your cheek, for you to carry in your dreams.

For O.

Everything welcomes you—thorny lizards,
the West Indian keeper of fighting cocks,
the fog caught in the throat of the valley.

They step towards you, or drift like airy continents,
for they know you are a conjurer of seeds,
of balances, and of the wind that shepherds them both.

Your lithe form cuts the sea open.
You spring melodies from cinnamon bark.
You mark everything with your eye, but impose no value.

Child, named after the fruit cured in oil and the salt
in its blood-brine, I wish only that you retain
the dignity of childhood, its vampiric dreams,

the thick scent of lilacs, the crayon's desire line,
and the others of your species, who, like you, sleep
with downed knots of the divine in their hair.

For W.

My difficult one, I love you for your difficulties,
the door that closes on your thumb, the strap that's too tight,
the root vegetable that retains too much rootiness.

Oceans rise in me when I watch your curled form sleep.
When you answer a stranger's question, you are a tamer
of inner lions. You release others' laughter the way

a conductor releases a tuba's belch.
I love how you stomp your foot at injustice
and then become sorrowful for your foot,

which you console with the salt of your tears.
All your premonitions will come true, which is why
I am grateful your intoxicating scent has thorns.

When I sing lullabies into your shell ears, the ocean
sings back, and you exhale dreams into the inch of air
between us. And when I cry, it is you who pats my back.

Joanna Solfrian

Ode to a Little One

Oh, fat little one orbiting
an invisible column
near my garage,
oh little gravitational pull, oh friend,
my eyes are round to your roundness,
your hairy geniality.

From a god's humble leftovers
you bubbled up;
he thought he'd mismade you,
little plummy beast, who has not
the aeronautics to fly,

but you don't mind, so
you fly.

Your wings, how many?
They hum and burr and bum bum bum
each time you stagger into
a new poppy.

Oh black and yellow demoted planet,
oh child's scoop of fuzzy cheek,

are you finding the poppy sweet and
do you know my sorrows?
Friends in the sky and friends in the ground,
the sad shadows of middle age,

a loosening equator,
the unappeasable organ, and a girl
with a sun for a crown

who will no longer hold my hand.

But you, sorrowless bumblebee,
you bumble in mid-air, too low to luxuriate
with the angels, too high to stint
with the seeds,

though you are friend to both,
with your wings god-glued to your back
and your tumescent, expectant belly—

oh bee, why will she not hold my hand?

Madness

Last night, madness came to the door dressed as a custodian. I led him up the dark stairs to the kitchenette to show him the copper stain, the leak. Instead he sat and asked for coffee, hands resting on crossed knees. His suit was worn but clean. I filled the pot from the faucet, lit the burner, and while the crows outside interpreted he explained that genius was sporadic, and not for everyone. The coffee was bitter, as was to his liking. There was no cat. After several minutes we had become as old lovers: no lust, but fondness, as of bookshelves. He said, tomorrow, same time? Sanity will occupy you in the morning.

The Red Guest

Then all at once the red guest unmoored. He commanded
his one-man processional through tunnels, sudden corners,
and wide-open pools, adjusting his shape as need be. The gray
Eden appealed most, so off he sailed. The other guests grew
fainter in their noises ... something about multiplication tables,
sunfish, what a snooze. He was number one! In the gray Eden,
streams slowed and lay still in their beds. Doors shut, chairs up
and left. This was not according to plan! He went mad with
logic. Where was his audience? Why did the Eden reject his
immaculate nude? His heart (the one he imagined) was full
of magic oil that no one wanted. So he raged. And in his rage
he grew. The walls closed in, a fault in perception. He wanted
to suffer *everywhere!* He wanted to find the spot where lightning
bolts were fashioned! He wanted to open the word-box
to Gesù Bambino! Most of all, he wanted to turn the wheel
that quickened the pulse when Big Papi shot another star
into the sky. The host would share these things, if he could,
because the host was just that way. But rage inflamed
the red guest—the host wasn't sharing *fast* enough!
So he made the throat stop swallowing. He froze
the left arm, then the left leg. And worst of all,
he ate up sound. Gone was speech, gone was
the melody, gone were the words that might
have said something of love. Thinking he'd won,
the guest bloated with pride.
                              But what he didn't know
was that the host had been a magician. The host had held
several birthday parties, had tricks up his thrift-store

sleeve. One of them involved a door, and a volunteer.
This was the trick the host pulled now,
only this time, he was the magician,
and the volunteer.

Fuck You, S., My Child's Bully

My child slept
with her mouth open
By the pink light I peeked
in her mouth

I was expecting roses
a tiny swingset
a gentle blue wave
I saw all of those things

But a boy sat
on the swings
with a stack of drawings

he chanted
"this is W. drowning!"
"this is W. buried alive!"
"this is W. getting stabbed!"

and I knew then she
had swallowed
the world

And the sum
of my existence
the threadbare cloud
of my skirt
my spine and its rectitude

sat on a separate
swingset
in a separate
childless
country

I prayed to the elements
and kissed as much fire
as I could summon
into her mouth

Toddler, I Love You

The capacity to feel is good to have; you know
you're a human when you feel relief that the keys
dropped down the storm grate; now you can skip
the mole removal and the grocery store. Having
feelings allows us to feel superior to the animals,
a ridiculous height to anyone who's ever witnessed
a dog. He's home! He's home! He's home!
Philosophers talk about the ontological thrust
of feelings, but they still get eczema. The toddler
covers her eyes and sings *you can't find me!*
and then yells at you when you do.
She's sitting on the couch, the sun to her
cheese stick and Highlights orbiters. You can shriek
your brains out at a toddler if you feel like it,
or you can discuss the feeling of wanting to shriek
your brains out with your spouse who probably
doesn't feel like it, which is just as well since
he hasn't emptied the dishwasher in days.
You are late writing a valentine and there's
a feeling of loneliness. You read Dean Young
and feel a lawyerly irritation at the gods who
should have let him bed Tsvetaeva so the whole
respective cardiologic and suicidal mess could've
been scotched. No one bedding anyone else
changes the physics of a rock lobbed at the sea.
There are no ordinary feelings; sure, I buy that.
A feeling: you think you're smarter than your
analyst and then Whoomp, There It Is: a stooped

43

and graying woman in snow boots with her back
turned to you, and there you go, quaking
in the clementines. Feeling, you'll never stop
sidling up uninvited, with no bottle to slake
the shaking throat. Last night, I dreamed
she soothed my brow and said *no, sweetie,*
I didn't die, and then the feeling
upon waking that yes, she did.

Bar Ghazal With Night Sky

Why ask where I traveled from with my sad face?
Don't you know a green-eyed lady doesn't hide the devil?

I've already cast roses into the sea.
I've watched mothers throw whole bouquets.

My book angers a man who says reading is high-falutin'.
Later, bloodshot, he rubs a woman against my rental car.

So many reasons to be done with stars, even the ones
God kicks-the-can with across the equatorial sky.

This is the year I cast out the planet that lives in my stomach.
Man at the bar slurring his Corona—look out.

Annaberg, St. John

Here is the table, the bread, the bowl of oranges.
Here are the two children, asleep in the ample sun.
The matted donkeys, simple as pebbles,
press their noses, soft as flour, into our palms.

Here is the water, a balm, consoling with its tears.
Here are your two hands—two scarred, white fish—
plucking the children from the rough waves, which delight.
Here is the sugar plantation, the tourists, the comfortable
    shoes.

Here are the ruins, the copper pot, the stone base of the
    windmill.
On Anna's Hill the children turn cartwheels. Here is the
    day-moon:
lone witness to the horses' plodding, the molasses blistering
in the copper pot, the windmill's stately rotation.

And the slaves, who warrant all poems, are the *jumbies*—
    ghosts—
who haunt this plantation, who speak with no translation,
who weep while the palm fronds soothe. Here is the sugar
    plantation,
the skeleton quarters, the tourists in comfortable shoes.

From a Boat, Scattering

Little companion shadow
you have grown long with grief.

I see you stretch from me
as the sun scolds, but you remain

at your base, stuck.
Your travel is infinitely limited.

I can't release you elsewhere,
you are mine, you suffer against me.

You need another companion
to play with! Where is the one

from the kindly giant?
He released it, cut it free—

don't stretch for these fraudulent friends
that by my hand fall …

they will dissolve, ignore, for
they are bone-clouds for sea beasts,

the ones no one can see
but we are told exist.

The Swing

Between earth and heaven
sleep has constructed a swing

and back and forth between the two
the not-mind sways.

In which place did you kill your brother?
Brick a new city, become queen?

Somehow, you plummeted
into childhood and reached up

a great distance to a hand. Vestal white,
your sandals against the pavement;

the sun ricocheted off the leather
and slapped your face with awe.

It doesn't matter the days,
their length, their offices …

the eyes again lie down
and the swing has her child.

Some nights it's a meadow.
Others, wolves.

Then they all die and the chain snaps—

and there you dangle,
hanging on for dear life.

3.

[dream]

When I curse my body, my god asks,
Why do you make a bed for perfection?

*It is a rude guest, souring its face
at all but your wine.*

But I have no more wine, I tell my god.
Jo, he says, *there are other medicines,*

and hands me a pencil. *This is for digging,*
he says, and I stand for a moment, staring.

Joanna Solfrian

Kane Street

while the streetlamps
are still lit
and it is warm and dark
in a normal sort of way

I will take your hand
and lead you to
the rug

we will lie down
like mountains
we will be massive
with streams and groves and roots

my knees will lift like stars
to your shoulders
and you will bow your head
because I am female

yes I am female
I am a goddamn mountain

with streams and groves and roots
oh and stars
that rest lightly

oh—
lightly—

on your shoulders

Joanna Solfrian

Instead of a Victorian Novel I Write a Victorian Poem

There is always a man,
slight and dark-socketed, standing by a window,
gazing at the mute and luminous moon.

Always the room is chandeliered,
warm at the center, and the conversation falls
in glitters like snowflakes and their infinitesimal knives.

The man wishes to speak to someone.

Always in the room there is a woman
radiating from her bones
who wants nothing but the man's loneliness
projected onto her palms.

Most often, neither speaks.

The woman remains on her spot of circumference,
her constructed worlds trembling in her breast,

and the man remains at the window,
slinging his losses at the moon.

Who can advise these two?

The moon, from her judicial height,
is the only one with any sense,
and everyone knows the moon can do nothing.

Ode to an Ash Can

We are having
a staring contest,
the ash can and I.
The fact that it has
no eyes
does not stop
the ash can.
Its lid, a gentlemanly,
flattened hat,
covers the eyes
that are not there.

O ash can!
You are winning.
Your organs are
consistent, although
originally disparate—
newspaper, scrub pines,
that black locust
that realized lightning
was the wrong
god.

The flames,
greedy prestidigitators,
stuffed themselves
to outdo your
complacent shine

but their bellies
never filled.
Ash floated up
and the flames cried
and waved their arms.

Then the ash
fulfulled its ash
destiny
and fell.
The fire retreated
like a Greek chorus
like thousands
of tiny witches dying
like the name
of the boy
with the dark eyes
and if not his name
then the feeling of
the name's kiss.

But this is about
the ash can!

You are trapezoidal
in section.
Fairly unromantic.
Practically-handled,

a never-burper.
Your sides are immune
to the ember's
goldfish bites.

Your pregnancy will
never develop.
You will never
groan, get up
and stomp out,
huffing, "I'm done
with this gig."
Ash can, you stay
an ash can.

And for this,
we do not thank you,
even though
night after night
you spare our home,
our sleep, our children,
our capacity to weep,
our eyes, and how,
when we stare at your
mute, armored breast,
they shift ever so
barely
each time

our heart
pinballs blood,
hoses us out
from the inside.

Joanna Solfrian

In the Margin

of a book
of sacred poems
about Sophia,
the divine female
at the center
of everything
who'd been written
out of Biblical
memory
by the male
hand,

you find a note
from an old self
that reads

ask Dad

and you didn't,
and you can't.

Elegy: Cribbage With Father

He comes to visit   in dreams
Last night,   he held my hand,
his legs were spry   like pegs
for the space   of the dream

Master of the arcane,
the invisible
mathematics—
he sat, cards arrayed

                           I am his child
in a quiver. He   delighted at sums
of certain power   He comes to visit.
Fifteen, thirty-one,
I am neither   In dreams
I am forty,   I am eight.
Unpaired.

No twilight yet   Sinking in his eyes
No traitorous bloom   on a hospital computer
In his speech   there is speech.

He was a
magician of rectangles,   He snap-shuffled
hearts, spades, more   hearts: then nothing. A
                           lunar light-step,
He beamed home—

and now inhabits   his number of months gone—
somewhere.
He keeps growing
in his distance,
too fast for even   The original entity
a fifteen, a thirty-one.

Hearts, then a spade   buried
In the king,   an axe in the head.

Who comes to me   In dreams

                           who is this
pure, invisible
                           unlonely wing?

Fun-O-Rama

York Beach, Maine

Jo, quit being sad; the fortune teller
is broken. Now no one knows if you'll get
that letter next Tuesday, the one that says
who torched the old hotel. No one knows
which waltz played while the flames ate
the alcohol. Jo, asthmatic, sleepy Jo,
your husband lies next to you and snores
like a carnie after a romp with the Bearded Lady.
Your mind-train follows a golden thread
through nightmares: merry-go-rounds spin
from the thumb of a listless giant,
an alabaster mannequin knifes your throat.
At four a.m. the circus will walk the elephants
down Main Street, and the elderly will sniff
the air for coffins. The elephants will spy
the sea and within their cells will awaken
some prehistoric need. Jo, bust the clown's
teeth with the black rubber ball. Squirt
the plastic ducks through the hunter's mouth.
Whack the heads of the id-obsessed alligators.
This is it: the world is the present tense.
Everyone has the same amount of time.
You feel in your bowels the dip
of the floorboards—the elephants
are coming. The dust in your room hovers
over your notebook, your pen—
what will you do, Jo, with your time?

Joanna Solfrian

My Friend Lt. Col. Aaron O'Connell E-Mails Me a Link and Says Everyone Deserves a Love Poem

for Marissa Gaeta and Citlalic Snell, who shared the Navy's first same-sex kiss at a ship's homecoming

Months on this damn ship with no one to console,
but tomorrow I return to shore.

Around your finger I put a diamond.
The earth gave up one of its stars for me.

I love you as a warrior is to be loved, straightforwardly;
I'm not fogged by your dark beauty, your full mouth.

Your full mouth! I turn to my weapons for order.
Their instruments obey me. The clock doesn't.

Are the flames in my thighs different from others'?
Why would they leap from me to someone's sacred text?

All love is a wished-for child. Tomorrow,
I will kiss you in front of thousands.

The Circumference of Time

Each day of their lives together a hand
from a great height erased a line.

The day the last line was erased, the man
stepped onto the porch to toss seeds to the birds.

An ordinary afternoon, until his heart turned
to the great height and seized

all that he loved in its chambers:
the schoolroom, the algorithms, the woman—

and the birds, his stewards
until the police came.

In his grave, it doesn't matter. Each February,
the man and the woman write their names on a tablecloth.

When he leans over to touch her hand, a bird wings
to the window of St. Valentine's cell,

a heart-shaped leaf in its beak. The saint traces a love note
on what the trees let go.

Joanna Solfrian

Now That the Children Are Grown

after Patrizia Cavalli

and time seems wrapped up and bowed
now that no one calls me to wipe excrement
and I can watch out the window
the scattered congregation of crows
now that there is no one to dress and undress
and snap and tie and dress and undress
and the weeds sprout flowers atop their stalks
now that there are no more sweet loaves of bellies
and I can climb in a vehicle and curse at highways
now that the evening rolls over and yawns obtusely
and no one cries out with fever and I can sit
fully within myself and pretend
to care about the transformative weeds
now that every word I dig up
can be held and weighed like a potato
suddenly I am fond of earthworms
and their professional urges.

After Drinking All Night With a Friend I Become Her and Write a Poem

You may think this is an old denim shirt
and skirt that falls white to the ankle,

but you are wrong—it is the sea, stitched by snails;
it is moonlight, glued by the weeping hands

of leaves. Look closely, friend, at the mud strung
on the spider's silk—these are not eyelashes.

I have drunk enough from the master's cup
to know that beholding the earthworm's waste

is not the work of the lonely
but of one whom others think is lonely.

Joanna Solfrian

The Tree Becomes a Ship

after John Haines

When men want to reach
faraway places,
they split me.

They tie canvas to my trunk,
ropes to my branches,
and yawp mighty orders
from where the wrens
once slept.

My roots and hollows
are left for the forest-child
who stows away secrets,
a toy gun.

The closest the men come
to longing is when they gaze
at the sea's bosom
and dream of women.

This they do
from the parts of me
that hold them up.

When they sleep in my hull,
my split core weeps
and I drop dead leaves
into their dreams.

Thinking of Rumi's "The Jar With the Dry Rim" After Seeing a Photo on the News Wire

for Alan Kurdi

Yes, the words are consolation;
    yes, each of us is a cup

and soon we will fill and
    sink, and not one bubble will lift

the ocean's meniscus—but the boy
    had a plan. He was going to eat

a slice of *sfia* and play
    in the yard with that dog.

There's no more bread. The monsters
    burned the dog.

And the ocean, which was supposed
    to hold the ship, got bored

and rolled the boy over and over
    until the sand took him.

Psalm Ghazal II

Touch the cheek of a child and God comes in through the
      fingers.
Open your mouth, and the devil comes in or the devil goes out.

Flatter with your tongue the wine and then the hollow inside
      my hip.
At the request of your lips, my mourning turns to dancing.

Only those who do not share their wine have enemies.
I have extra wine; no one is plotting my death but I.

You have always heard the words of my groaning.
At the gates of death, wait for me. And for the clear bell.

Joanna Solfrian

Guest

Once near a sea there lived a wind. The wind fell in love with the sea and its constant graces, the way it slept and heaved and reflected, the way fishes and moonlight swam in its generous graves. The wind wanted to share with the sea some of its own delights. Small towns and their steeple bells, the skirts of lovely women, and of course, the roads of the black whale who leapt to say hello. So the wind swept up armfuls of droplets and carried them to the small towns, where some atomized over the bells, or evaporated at the sight of the women. Then the wind carried the remaining droplets back to the sea to greet the whales. But each time they returned, the remaining droplets huddled and fell. The wind grieved and repeated its attempts to clutch the sea until the sky was filled with clouds.

And in this way the woman in the boat scattering ashes could not tell which were tears and which were rain.

Mass

the dead

held
the ones it had chosen

young girls
small, small children

the city has sustained

a rare
vision

elderly men talking
under the shade of a neem tree

begin
distributing

open-air prayers

an erasure poem from the article "Nigerians Who Fled Boko Haram Tell of Massacres Ruled by Whim," New York Times, *Friday, Feb. 6, 2015*

Joanna Solfrian

It Is True I Wish to Be an Ecstatic

I have sisters in the church.
When they sing they are immortal.
I know in what a flawed way
they bend their knees,
and God moves through them

when they are still, like pines.

My own God is a whisper.
When I wake in my dark city
and bend to tie my shoes,
I extend an ear to the dark roots.
Sometimes I hear.

Notes

"Toddler, I Love You," is a response to Dean Young's "Rabbit, I Love You." It includes two italicized lines from his poem: "The capacity to feel is good to have" and "There are no ordinary feelings."

"The Swing" begins with a variation on a theme by Kabir, from his poem of the same name.

"The Mud Room" is for the Wilkins-Lombardo family; "The Circumference of Time" is for Phyllis Isley; "For O." is for Olive Solfrian; "For W." is for Willa Solfrian (who is out of the toddler stage and is therefore not difficult); "After Drinking All Night With a Friend I Become Her and Write a Poem" is for Jennie Panchy.

All love poems are for Scott Solfrian.

ACKNOWLEDGMENTS

Grateful acknowledgment to the journals and anthologies that published the following poems, sometimes in altered form:

The Atlanta Review: "Guest"

Boulevard: "Annaberg, St. John"

Gargoyle Magazine: "Don't Come to Me With Your Whole Body"

The Harvard Review: "Now That the Children Are Grown"

Heroes Are Gang Leaders Gianthology: "Waiting for the Bus, Columbia Street, Brooklyn, the Day After the Writer Jumped Off the Staten Island Ferry," and "Fuck You, S., My Child's Bully"

High Window: "The Moon Has Come to My Window, So I Practice Gratitude," "The Mud Room," "After Drinking All Night With a Friend I Become Her and Write a Poem," "Ode to an Ash Can," and "The Trunk"

Image: "Psalm Ghazal I" and "Psalm Ghazal II"

The Missouri Review: "Travel"

Rattle: "Instead of a Victorian Novel I Write a Victorian Poem"

Rocked by the Waters: Poems of Motherhood, eds. Margaret Hasse & Athena Kildegaard (Nodin Press, 2020): "For W."

Salamander: "Anniversary"

Solstice Literary Magazine: "For O."

Thank you to the following readers, friends, and mentors for their insights and encouragement: Jennie Panchy, Dzvinia Orlowsky, D. Nurkse, Baron Wormser, and the February Poem-A-Day group.

Thank you also to The Lamothe House in New Orleans, LA, whose staff made sure I had a desk.

ABOUT THE AUTHOR

JOANNA SOLFRIAN's first book, *Visible Heavens*, was chosen by Naomi Shihab Nye for the 2009 Stan and Tom Wick Prize, a national first book award. Her poems have appeared in journals such as *The Harvard Review, Boulevard, Rattle, Salamander, Margie, The Southern Review, Pleiades, Image,* and also in the internationally-touring art exhibit *Speak Peace: American Voices Respond to Vietnamese Children's Paintings.* She is a graduate of the Stonecoast MFA program, a MacDowell fellow, and a four-time Pushcart Prize nominee. Joanna lives and works in New York City. www.joannasolfrian.com

www.ingramcontent.com/pod-product-compliance
Lightning Source LLC
Chambersburg PA
CBHW021421090426
42742CB00009B/1204